CW00404935

HOW TO STREET FIGHT

STREET FIGHTING TECHNIQUES FOR LEARNING SELF-DEFENSE

SAM FURY

Illustrated by
NEIL GERMIO

WARNINGS AND DISCLAIMERS

The information in this publication is made public for reference only.

Neither the author, publisher, nor anyone else involved in the production of this publication is responsible for how the reader uses the information or the result of his/her actions.

CONTENTS

GROUND FIGHTING

WEAPONRY

THANKS FOR YOUR PURCHASE

Did you know you can get FREE chapters of any SF Nonfiction Book you want?

https://offers.SFNonfictionBooks.com/Free-Chapters

You will also be among the first to know of FREE review copies, discount offers, bonus content, and more.

Go to:

https://offers.SFNonfictionBooks.com/Free-Chapters

Thanks again for your support.

INTRODUCTION

How to Street Fight is a simple, unrefined, close range, and aggressive fight training system which you can build upon at your own will.

It contains techniques and training methods, while at the same time being a strategic fighting guide. Using words and simple pictures, it describes strikes, takedowns, grappling, ground fighting, weaponry, defensive techniques, and more. The information in it is intended to be used in three ways:

1. As a fun and interesting way to keep fit.
2. For self-defense/a street fight. When all other methods of escape have been exhausted and fighting is unavoidable, only use as much force as is needed in order for you to escape.
3. To help you escape from a life-threatening situation. Attack in full force until you have incapacitated your opponent(s).

Note: It is up to you to decide what information and how much force is appropriate to use in any situation. Eye and groin attacks are not suitable for sparring, for example.

The techniques in this book are presented in the order you should learn them according to strategy. Please remember that they are not to be used lightly. When training, please be careful, and if you have to use them in a real street fight (hopefully you are never in such a situation), please be mindful of your use of force. In most cases, it is best to not fight.

SAFETY

Follow these guidelines to get the most out of training and do so safely.

- Use proper equipment (mats, training weapons, protective equipment, etc.) where applicable.
- Wear appropriate clothing and no jewelry.
- Train for reality, but only use enough force to get the desired effect.
- Put safety before pride. "Tap out" before you need to.
- Don't train when you have injuries.
- Get injuries checked out by a professional ASAP to prevent them from getting worse.
- Ensure you are physically ready before you begin training. If you have any doubts, see your physician.
- Warm up, cool down, and stretch.

TRAINING METHODS

Shadowboxing

Shadowboxing is practicing to fight against an imaginary enemy. It needs no equipment (although a mirror can be useful). Do it slowly to learn/improve technique or increase speed for a warmup or an aerobic workout. Imagine a scenario, such as fighting multiple opponents, and react as you should according to the strategy.

Reaction Training

In this method, one person attacks and the other person reacts. It can be combined with pad work. The parameters of attack and response are decided upon beforehand, and protective equipment should be considered.

Sparring

To spar is to fight against one or more partners for training purposes. Conditional variations are limited only to your imagination (hands only, feet only, eyes closed, anything but weapons, just ground fighting, first to take down, first to get the weapon, anything goes, etc.).

Start slowly. As skills improve, you can increase speed. As fitness builds, you can increase timed rounds.

Only go as hard/fast as the least experienced fighter can safely go. This may be dictated by the more experienced fighter if they feel that their sparring partner is going harder/faster than they can safely control.

Note: Your power level is totally separate from your aggressiveness level. You can still be at 100% aggressiveness while only using 20% power.

Protective equipment is highly recommended.

Tapping Out

Tapping out is something you can do when you submit/give up, such as when a lock starts to hurt. Tap your opponent at least twice, so that he feels it. He must disengage immediately. If you cannot reach your opponent, tap the floor. You can also use a verbal tap-out, like "stop."

Pad/Bag Work

With or without a partner, practice techniques on a punching bag or pads (pillows, mattresses etc. can be low-cost substitutes). Pad/bag work allows you to hit something hard.

When you are sparring, strikes are often pulled back to prevent injury. This trains you not to hit hard. You can hit hard in shadowboxing, but you are not actually hitting anything, so you do not get the full effect. Pad/bag work is the answer.

Related Chapters:

- Achieving Maximum Power
- Fighting Multiple Opponents

ACHIEVING MAXIMUM POWER

> "If you have unshakable balance, correct technique, pinpoint accuracy, lightning speed and incredible force, you will naturally create awesome power."
>
> **Bruce Lee**

Keep your balance while upsetting your opponent's. Correct technique will ensure this. Strengthen your balance in everyday life by skipping on each foot, standing on one foot while doing things, etc.

First, learn the technique and proper form in a relaxed manner.

Aim at a recommended target area. Aim 3 inches behind your target.

Increase your speed of movement while maintaining your force. This can be done through repetitive training and muscle conditioning, including stretching. Stay relaxed until the last moment before the impact of the strike.

Target Areas

A good target area is one that will cause sufficient pain and/or disablement when struck, even if the strike is not incredibly forceful. It also needs to be easy to hit, and not a pinpoint target.

Point of chin. A good strike here can knock someone out, and if you miss, then at least you are hitting him in the face.

Eyes. If you attack a person's eyes aggressively, it can do permanent damage.

Neck/throat. The neck and/or throat can be attacked with strikes or chokes.

Lower torso. This includes abdomen, lower ribs and solar plexus.

Groin. Attacking the groin is effective on all genders.

Base of the skull. A good strike here can knock someone out.

Base of the spine. Striking here is excessive, but may be necessary in a life-threatening situation.

Legs. If you take out your opponent's legs, he cannot get up to attack you. When you are fighting someone who is not conditioned, striking anywhere in his leg (including his feet) can cause pain.

Joints. Knees, elbows, shoulders, fingers etc. Apply pressure in the opposite direction from the one the joint was meant to go in. Apply it slowly for compliance. Apply it swiftly and/or increase pressure to break the joint.

Related Chapter:

- Training Methods

FIGHTING ON YOUR FEET

YOUR FIGHTING STANCE

At the first sign of confrontation, adopt the fighter's position (FP).

Your Lead Side

If your right leg is forward-most, then your right side is your lead and your left side is your rear.

Train on both sides, but when fighting, have your strong side as your lead most of the time. Most of your strikes will come off your lead.

Fighter's Position (FP)

Initially, the FP appears non-aggressive, but it leaves you primed for attack and defense.

Stand with your feet shoulder-width apart and take a natural step back. Put a slight bend in your knees. Your body should be relaxed, with a slight forward lean.

Note: You step back because it is a non-aggressive gesture. If your intention is to attack as you adopt the FP, then step forward to close distance and strike.

Find the point at which you are most balanced. To test that, have someone push you from the front.

Your hands should come up near your head, with your lead hand slightly forward. Keep your palms open, facing in at each other, and about half-facing your opponent. Keep your elbows in close to your body.

When engaging, keep your teeth together, chin tucked, and eyes up.

THE BEST WAY TO WIN A FIGHT... FAST!

Attacking first, fast, hard, and by surprise is the best way to win a street fight. Attack your opponent when he is not ready, and then keep attacking until you have won.

You have won when your opponent is no longer trying to attack you. This could be because he has given up or you have rendered him physically unable to fight. Take advantage whenever he gets distracted, including while either of you is talking.

Beware of Telegraphing

Anything you do that alerts your opponent to your intentions is telegraphing. Show no sign of preparation for movement.

How to Sneak Up On Someone

The best way to prevent telegraphing is to attack from behind. Some may look down on this tactic, but you may wish to do this if someone is attacking a friend, if someone is looking to harm you but hasn't found you yet, etc. Move swiftly and quietly. If possible, crouch down to come in below your target's eye level.

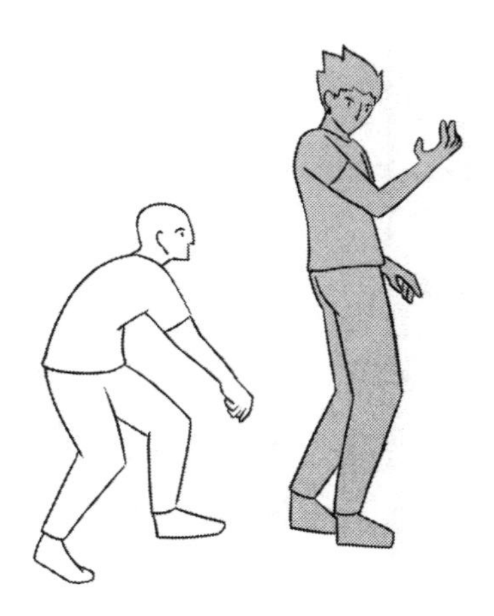

REAR NAKED CHOKE

The rear naked choke (RNC) can cause unconsciousness within 10 seconds. The resumption of consciousness is as fast.

Encircle your opponent's neck with your right arm. His trachea should be in the crook of your elbow. Your right hand should grab your upper left arm, preferably at the bicep.

Put your left hand behind his head and squeeze your elbows together.

If Your Opponent Tucks His Chin

Force your opponent to expose his neck by pulling up at his eyes or scraping your forearm under his nose.

Applying the RNC On a Tall Opponent

Either jump off the ground to grab his neck or cut him down—by attacking his groin, for example—then apply the RNC.

If you have at least some hold of him, you can stomp on the back of his knee and/or walk backwards to lower him.

Note: As a general rule in all fighting, never show your back to an opponent.

Applying any choke for longer than necessary may lead to brain damage or even death. Prevent this by releasing your opponent or training partner as soon as he goes limp or taps out. If he is unconscious for more than 20 seconds, seek medical help.

Encourage the resumption of consciousness by lifting his legs so the blood goes back to his head.

Related Chapter:

- Training Methods

STRIKING YOUR OPPONENT FROM BEHIND

The best place to strike someone from behind is at the base of the skull. This gives the best chance for a knockout. Use a blunt weapon or your palm heel.

Palm Heel

The palm heel is used instead of the fist to prevent damage to yourself. Some arm reach is lost, but the sacrifice is worth it.

Pull your fingers back out of the way and make contact using the lower part of your palm.

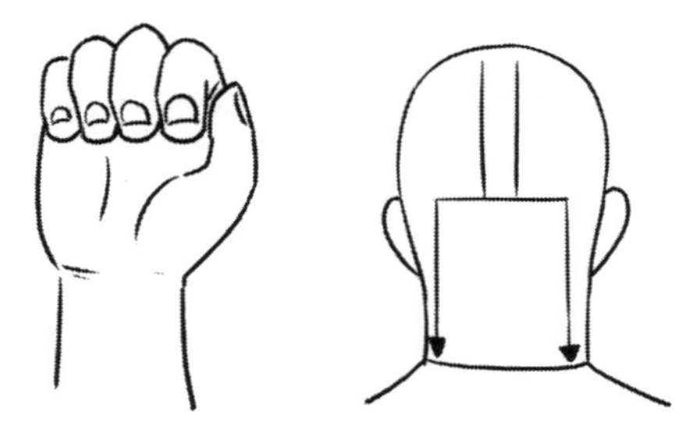

Strike your opponent with as much power as you can at the base of his skull (where the top of his neck meets the bottom of his head). Put your weight behind the strike.

If the strike does not knock him out, rush him or apply the RNC.

Related Chapters:

- Achieving Maximum Power
- Rear Naked Choke
- Rushing Your Opponent

RUSHING YOUR OPPONENT

To "rush" is to quickly close in on your opponent with a flurry of attacks, with the intent of finishing the fight.

Quick Advance

Use the quick advance to quickly close distance and/or increase power in an attack.

When doing all footwork, have both knees slightly bent and relaxed. Keep your feet close to the ground and move swiftly. The distance between your feet should be as in your fighting stance whenever possible.

Step forward with your front foot approximately 3 inches. Immediately slide your rear foot to trail the lead.

When striking with the quick advance, move your hand first. The strike must hit its target before your lead foot lands; otherwise, you will lose power.

Related Chapters:

- Achieving Maximum Power
- Your Fighting Stance
- Positioning and Footwork

ELBOWS AND KNEES

Elbows and knees are fast and powerful fight-finishers. This is because they are harder and less fragile than the bones in the hand, and strikes using them can be delivered with much greater force.

Elbows

Begin in the FP. Twist your hip sharply and pivot on the ball of your foot (the foot on the same side as the elbow you are striking with). Snap and drive your elbow into your opponent's face, preferably his jaw.

Keep your hand open to expose the bone, your elbow close to your body, and your arm loose until the last moment. Your wrist should stay limp.

As in all strikes, power comes up from the ground and from the pivot in your hips.

For added power, grab your opponent and drive his head into your elbow as you strike.

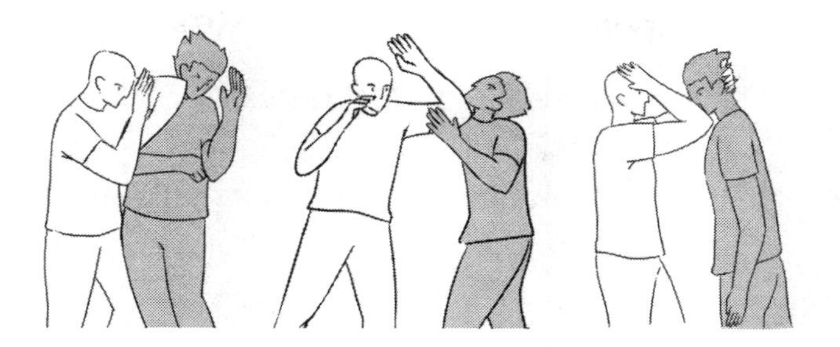

Knees

Knees can make contact from a variety of angles.

Pull your opponent's hair/head/ears down and drive your knee into his face.

Do it more than once consecutively for more damage.

Extend your hips and come up with your toes to increase your force. Point your foot and toes down for protection.

A knee to the groin is also very effective. If needed, hold your opponent's shoulders.

Related Chapters:

- Achieving Maximum Power
- Your Fighting Stance

ATTACK COMBINATIONS

A combination is any flowing sequence of attacks. Some examples are:

- Lead palm heel, rear palm heel (1-2)
- 1-2, grab, and elbow
- Elbows and knees
- 1-2, choke
- 1-2, elbows and knees, choke
- Elbows and knees, basic trip

1-2 Combination

The 1-2 combination is a lead palm heel, followed by a rear palm heel. In the rush, it is used to bridge the gap for the use of elbows/knees/chokes etc.

Note: All strikes can also be used individually.

Lead Palm Heel

From the fighter's position, strike straight out. Do not pull back before you strike.

Protect your head with your rear hand.

Strike through your opponent (not push), and then recover by bringing your limb straight back. Strike with your whole body. Transfer the force of your legs, waist and shoulder into the strike.

Rear Palm Heel

As you are retracting your lead, thrust your rear palm heel out through your target. Push off your rear foot and torque your hips as you strike. Bend your front leg and bring up your rear leg slightly while you're executing. Extend your rear shoulder to maximize the reach of your arm for penetrating power.

Related Chapters:

- Achieving Maximum Power
- Your Fighting Stance
- Rushing Your Opponent
- Elbows and Knees
- Putting Your Opponent On the Ground

THE THREE-SECOND KNOCKOUT

The person who gets the first good blow in has a much greater chance of winning the fight.

As soon as you sense the fight is inevitable, strike your opponent in the chin, preferably when he is not ready.

Take advantage whenever he gets distracted, including when either of you is talking.

Often, a good strike to the point of his chin will knock him out, but you should not just strike once in confidence that he will drop. Doing so will leave you vulnerable to counterattacks.

It is better to attack in combination with no initial intent to stop until you are sure you have won.

You have won when your opponent is no longer trying to attack you. This could be because he has given up or you have rendered him physically unable to fight.

Related Chapters:

- Achieving Maximum Power
- Attack Combinations
- Counters and Feinting

GUILLOTINE CHOKE

You may come up against a very tough opponent who will not be put by from your initial attack.

Continuing to strike aggressively for too long will cause fatigue and/or damage to you. If this happens, or before it happens, choke your opponent out.

Either move behind him and use the RNC, or use the guillotine from the front.

Wrap your arm around the back of your opponent's neck and under the front of it, so that his head is to the side of your torso. Your palm should facing your own chest. Ideally, your forearm will be under his Adam's apple.

Use your other hand to grasp your first hand/wrist/forearm, and then pull up into yourself with both hands.

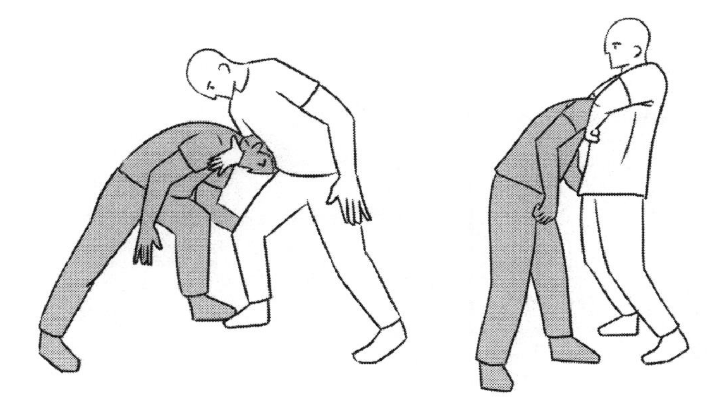

Related Chapter:

- Rear Naked Choke

LANDING SAFELY

Another option you have is to force your opponent onto the ground. But before training in takedowns, you must learn how to land safely.

Break-Falling

Break-falling is one method of safe landing. It "breaks" your fall by allowing you to take the impact on the meaty portions of your body.

Spread the force of the fall, relax your body, and slap the ground. Keep as much of your spine off the ground as you can, and protect your head by tilting it away from the ground.

Side Break-Fall

Swing your right arm and right foot across the center line of your body, collapsing your left knee. When you land, do so on as much of your right side as possible. Don't let your elbow hit and slap the ground hard. Your left foot should still be on the ground, and your knee should be folded.

As always, practice on the left side as well.

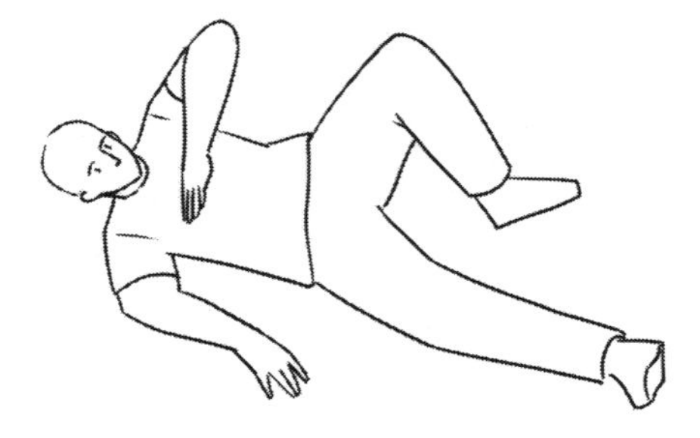

Back Break-Fall

Squat down to lower yourself closer to the ground.

Arch your back and thrust your groin up toward the ceiling while simultaneously slapping with both hands. Tuck your chin to your chest to protect your head. Make contact with the ground with your upper shoulders.

As your confidence increases, don't squat down so much.

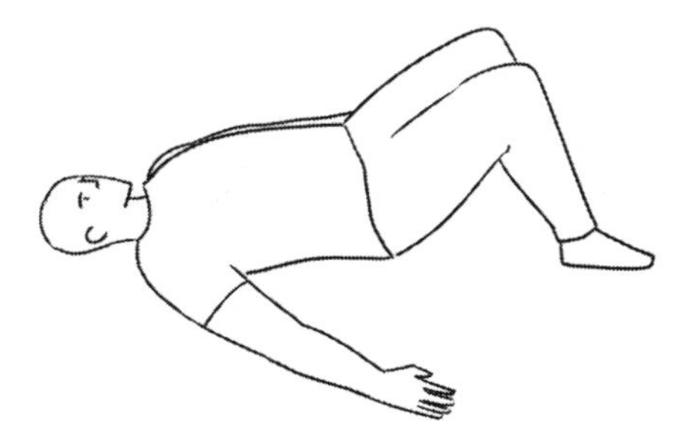

Forward Break-Fall

Squat down and fall forwards, landing on your forearms with your palms down. You should land in a planking position. Only your forearms and toes should be in contact with the ground.

Increase to falling from a standing position, then jumping, etc.

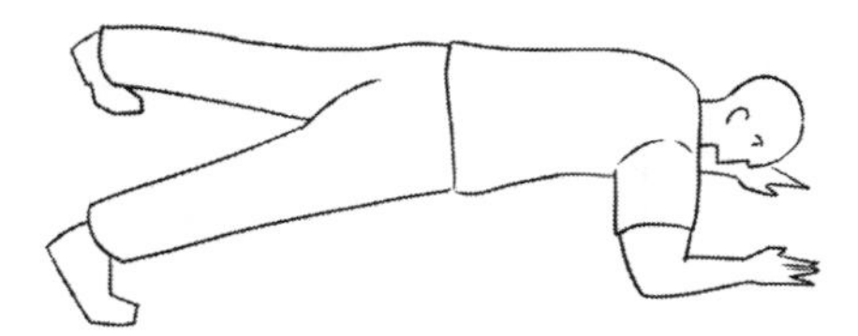

Rolling

In general, rolling is better than the break-fall because you will return to your feet.

Sometimes, due to the way you are being forced to the ground—when you're being tackled by the legs, for example—rolling is not possible, which is why you learn to break your fall.

Forward Roll

Put your right foot forward and make your right arm into a sturdy arc. Swing your right arm hard across your center line. Tuck your head and roll over your right shoulder.

The pressure should run from your right shoulder diagonally across your back, ending up somewhere around your left hip.

As you go over, bend your left knee, so that your momentum brings you back to your feet to face your opponent(s).

Backward Roll

As you are falling, tuck your chin and collapse your rear leg as if sitting down on your calf.

Keep your body curved and loose as you fall backwards and roll over the shoulder opposite the leg you collapsed.

Come out of the roll into the fighter's position to face your opponent(s).

Note: If falling back or to the side, you can side break-fall and then, if able, continue into the backward roll.

Forward Roll with Break-Fall

This is useful if there is something preventing you from completing the roll, such as a wall.

When you go into your roll, keep the side opposite your rolling arm perfectly rigid. Roll across your arm, shoulder, and lower hip. Slap hard to come to a sudden stop.

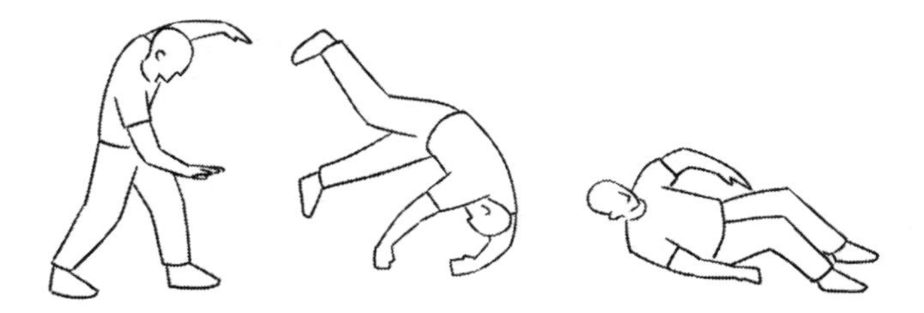

Related Chapter:

- Training Methods

PUTTING YOUR OPPONENT ON THE GROUND

Now that you know how to land safely, you can learn how to put your opponent on the ground. Here are some simple methods to take him down while you stay standing, which is always preferred.

Triangle Theory

Triangle theory is a basic balance concept. To put someone on the ground, you must upset his balance. Knowing this will also help you maintain your balance.

When you are standing, your feet make up two points of a triangle. The third point, which can be on either side, is the direction in which you are most off balance.

If you are forced towards this third point, you will be unbalanced. If you cannot reposition yourself to regain your balance, you will fall.

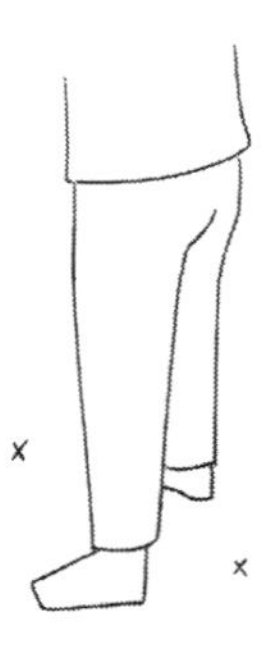

Basic Trip

Grab your opponent in a bear hug, by the shirt front, or by the shoulders, and bring him close.

Place your foot at his third point behind him, as close to his body as possible without losing your own balance.

Throw/shove him over your leg.

Twist Your Opponent's Head

Where your opponent's head goes, his body will follow.

Grab his head by the top and under his chin, and twist it towards the floor. You can combine this with the basic trip.

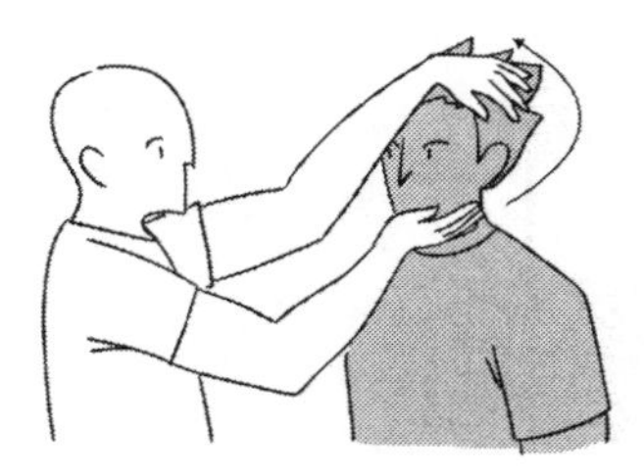

Once Your Opponent is On the Ground

Once your opponent is on the ground, stomp him and/or escape.

When attacking someone on the ground, come in from the side. Stomp his knees, ribs, and chest with the heel of your foot.

Stomping his head is excessive, but may be necessary in a life-threatening situation.

IF YOUR OPPONENT STRIKES FIRST

If your opponent makes the initial strike, there are a number of techniques/strategies you can use. The one you use will depend on the type of incoming attack and how quickly you are able to react.

Bursting

Bursting is best used against curved attacks like hooks.

Using the power from your legs, move forward explosively (not jumping), while blocking and striking at the same time. Your block and strike should land simultaneously.

Aim your strike (palm heel) at your opponent's chin or upper torso.

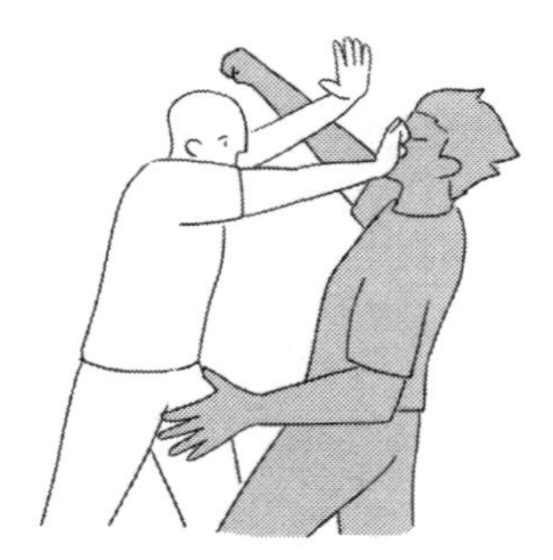

Slip, Parry, and Strike

This is one move with three components. It is best used against straight attacks like a jab, cross, or straight punch.

As the attack comes in, move your head to the outside of your opponent's striking arm and a little forward, so you can close in to attack.

Move it just enough to not get hit. This is the slip.

At the same time, use your hand to brush the strike off. This is the parry, and in this instance, it is used a secondary defense.

Only move your arm enough to redirect your opponent's strike away from you. It should not go past your shoulder.

If your slip is good, then you may not even make contact with the parry.

At the same time, with the hand that isn't parrying, palm heel your opponent.

Use the rush—that is, close in with a quick advance and then attack.

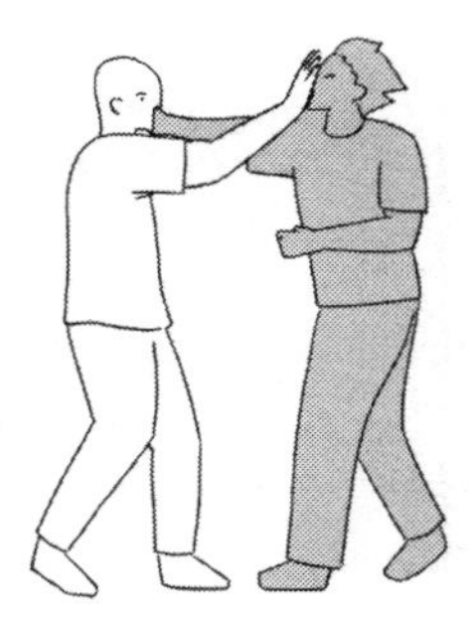

Cover and Rush

This is also for side attacks. Cover up and move into elbow and knee range to neutralize the impact of your opponent's strike(s). Then you will attack.

From the fighter's position, lift your elbows up and forward so that your palms are resting/pressing on your ears or forehead. Your elbows should be sticking out in front of you.

If you can, hold your forearms towards the direction of attack.

Keep your eyes up, your chin tucked, and your teeth together.

Use the quick advance to close in and rush your opponent.

Sprawling

This is a classic mixed martial arts (MMA) technique used to defend against someone tackling you.

As your opponent lunges towards you, kick your legs back and drop your weight onto his upper back.

Arch your back as much as possible, and stay on your feet/toes.

Apply the guillotine.

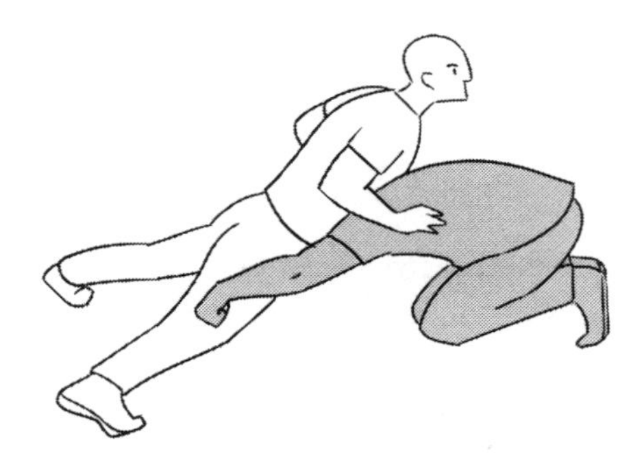

Related Chapters:

- Achieving Maximum Power
- Attack Combinations
- Rushing Your Opponent
- Guillotine Choke

FIGHTING ON

In some circumstances, a fight may go on over a minute. Some reasons for this may be:

- The fighters are evenly matched.
- The people fighting do not actually want to fight.
- Neither fighter is aggressive enough to finish the fight quickly.
- The fighters are sparring (a training simulation).

Whatever the reason, continuing to fight intensely will wear you out. You must "fight on" at a less intense pace until there is another opportunity to rush.

Note: If your opponent attacks first and you miss the rush opportunity, start fighting on.

ALWAYS FOCUS ON ATTACKING, WITH THE INTENTION OF WINNING.

Even when you are defending, you should be thinking of your attack. Defense is an aid to that. Always be on the attack. It is very important.

Parry, then attack. Move swiftly to avoid being struck, but keep pressing forward.

Related Chapters:

- Training Methods
- Rushing Your Opponent
- Slip, Parry, and Strike

POSITIONING AND FOOTWORK

Positioning

Use footwork and your surrounding environment to your full advantage. Some examples are:

- Force your opponent into awkward places.
- Adopt the higher ground.
- Position your opponent so that the sun/light/smoke is in his eyes.

Switching

Use a switch to change your lead side. It is handy for confusing in your opponent if he has gotten accustomed to your original lead, but is more commonly used when naturally flowing on after striking.

This is easily done by stepping through—when kicking or in combination, for example. A quick switch can be made by way of a little jump, made as low to the ground as possible.

Quick Retreat

The quick retreat is the same as the quick advance but in reverse. That is, you move your rear foot first.

Note: Never take more than three steps back unless you are sure you know what is behind you.

All Other Footwork

To make side, circular and diagonal movements, use the same principles as in the quick advance and retreat.

Keep balanced by keeping your feet low to the ground and maintaining the distance between your feet as best you can. Never cross them.

Related Chapters:

- Rushing Your Opponent
- Attack Combinations

FRONT KICKS

Lift your knee up as high as you want to aim (no higher than your opponent's groin), and angle it toward the target.

Snap your foot into the target using the ball, bottom, or heel of your foot.

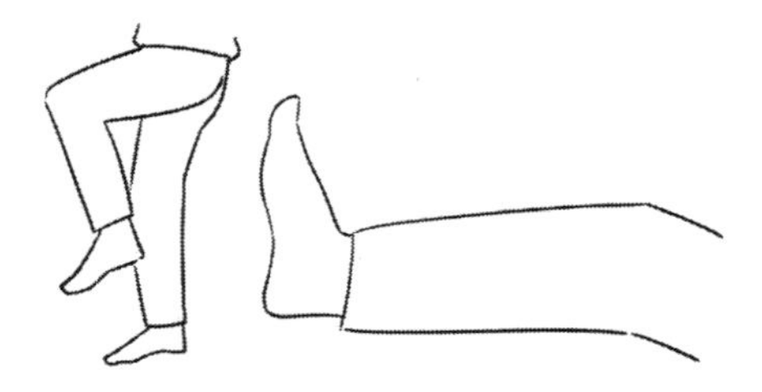

Move your foot back to the ground along the same path that you extended it.

Shins, knees, and the groin are the best targets.

Related Chapters:

- Achieving Maximum Power

DEFENSE AGAINST STRIKES

Dodging Strikes

If a strike is coming straight at your face and you can't burst or slip, parry, and palm heel, then move out of the way.

Combine this with parrying if needed. Use footwork and sharp movements from the waist.

Checking

The best defense against kicks is dodging. If dodging is not possible, or you want to close in, use the check. The check works especially well when defending against kicks coming in from the side, as in Muay Thai.

As the attack comes in, lift your leg perpendicular to your opponent's. Your shin bone should be turned towards his. It will hurt if you are not conditioned.

If you want to close, lean into the check so you step down towards him, and attack.

Note: The picture shows no intent of closing.

Defending Against Knees

Block your opponent's knee with your arms, and if/when possible, drop your elbow into his thigh as he brings his knee up. If needed, catch and hold onto his leg.

Related Chapters:

- Attack Combinations
- If Your Opponent Strikes First
- Positioning and Footwork

COUNTERS AND FEINTING

Counters

A counter is an attack in reply to an attack. A perfect example of this is the slip, parry, and palm heel.

If you parry and strike (counter) with different hands, then the two can be done simultaneously, like the burst.

If you parry and strike with the same hand, then strike from where you finish your parry.

Parrying and countering can also be done without your opponent throwing an initial attack. As you advance, parry his lead hand down and immediately follow up with a strike. This works especially well if he holds his guard out too far.

Feinting

Pretend to attack your opponent so that he reacts. By doing so, you can anticipate his response and counter.

The feint must be a real (although partial) attack, so he is convinced to react.

Note: Every movement you make should have a purpose. You should always strike for hits, whether they are direct hit, or attempts to deduce information. Don't waste energy on misses.

Related Chapters:

- Attack Combinations
- Rushing Your Opponent
- If Your Opponent Strikes First

IF YOU BECOME OVERWHELMED

You may become overwhelmed by your opponent. If so, go into the covering up position as described in cover and rush.

As soon as the opportunity arises, attack.

If there is no break, hug him tight, preferably around his arms, and then employ one or more of the following attacks and/or the basic trip.

Headbutt

Tilt your head slightly downward, clench your teeth, stiffen your neck muscles, and frown.

Take aim and lunge forward using your whole body (if possible).

Connect to your target with your forehead. Your opponent's nose is a good target.

Aim to strike using the area one inch or 25mm above your eyebrow.

To increase force, bend at the middle of your back and lean back a bit before striking.

Attack the Eyes

Your opponent's ability to fight will be drastically reduced if he cannot see, so obscure his vision. Put your thumbs in his eyes, throw dirt or sand in his face, move so that the sun in his eyes, etc.

Attack the Groin

Strike your opponent's groin with your knee. Even better, grab his groin and twist. Doing this causes much more pain than just hitting his groin.

Related Chapters:

- Achieving Maximum Power
- Putting Your Opponent On the Ground
- If Your Opponent Strikes First

ESCAPING SOMEONE'S GRIP

Use the following techniques when grabbed by surprise. Adjust your reaction to the severity of the situation.

Twist and/or Jerk

The weakest point on your opponent's hand is where his thumb meets his fingers. Manipulate it to escape his grip.

For example, if he grabs your right wrist, then in one swift movement bring your right hand up in a clockwise direction so your palm is facing your face.

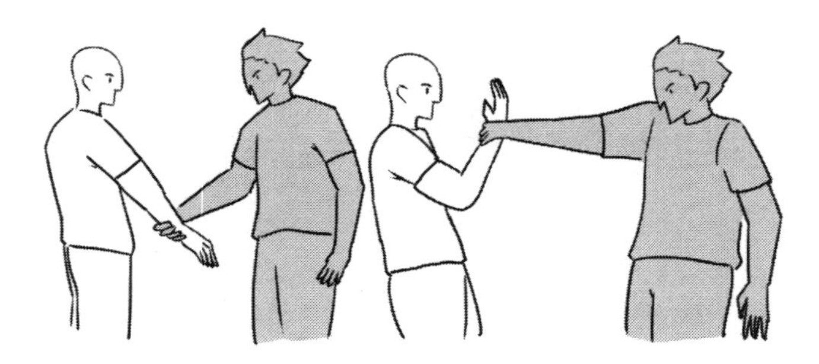

In the same movement, turn your thumb towards your face and thrust your hand down to the right to break his grip.

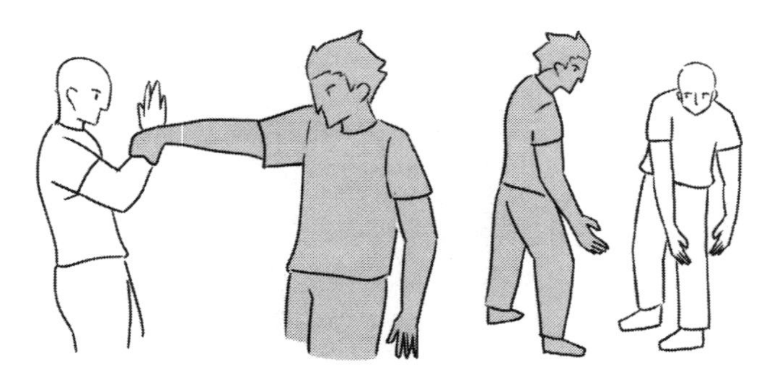

Hit Your Opponent's Forearm Mound

The forearm mound is a cluster of nerves.

Find the point halfway between your elbow and your wrist. Halfway between this point and your elbow is the forearm mound. You can see the muscle pop out when you clench your fist.

Hitting this point hard three to five times will make most people loosen their grip.

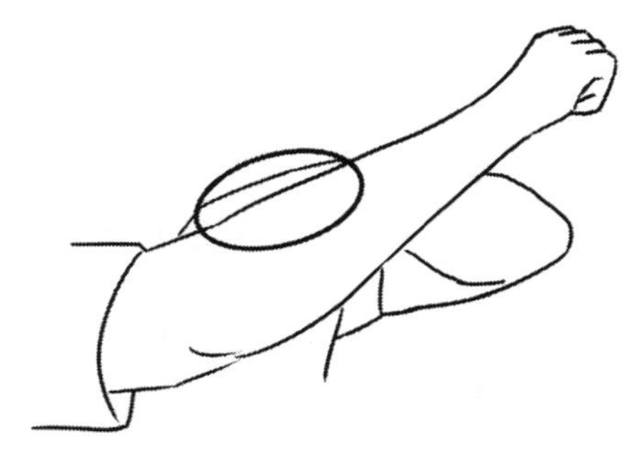

Bend Your Opponent's Fingers

If you get hold of one of your opponent's fingers, you can easily gain his compliance and loosen his grip.

Bending and twisting them back towards his wrist is most effective. The little finger is easiest to manipulate.

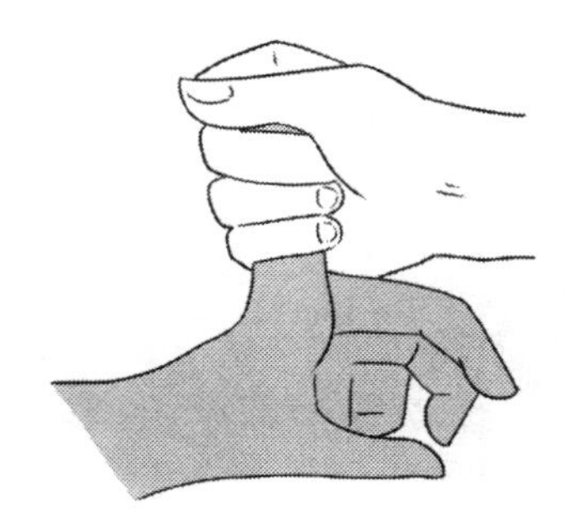

Finger Split

Grab two of your opponent's fingers in one hand, and the other two in your other hand. Separate them.

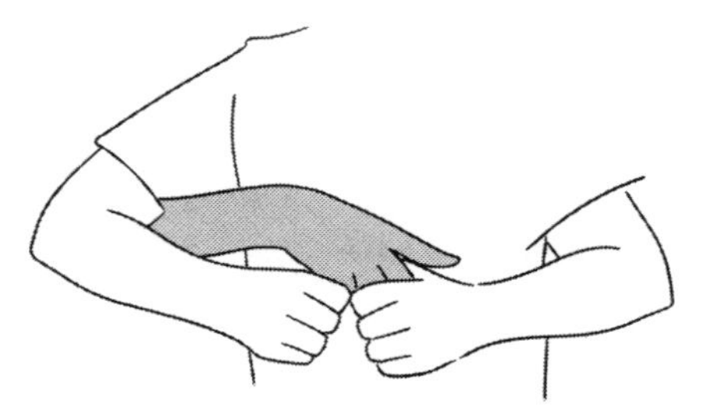

Attack the Back of Your Opponent's Hands

Use a pen or a similar object, such as a lighter, and strike the back of your opponent's hand, or place the object there and rub vigorously.

You could also use the lighter to burn his hand.

Scratch Your Opponent's Cuticle

Scratch your opponent at the point where the bottom of his finger nail meets his finger.

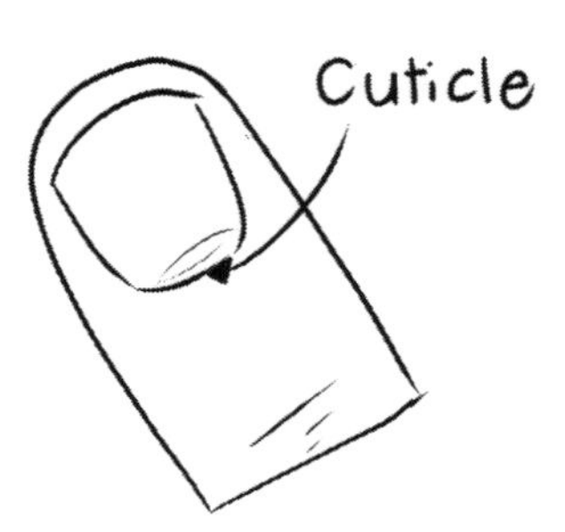

Bite Your Opponent

Beware of disease.

Shaking your head while you bite will cause more pain.

Escaping a Bear Hug

A bear hug is a move in which someone wraps his arms tightly around you with the intent of restricting your movements.

Your basic defense is to loosen his grip enough to face him, attack aggressively, and then escape when you can.

ATTACKING TO YOUR REAR

Back Elbow

You can drive your elbow straight back from your waist into your opponent's lower torso or in a rear hooking motion at his head.

Back Heel

Use this move on your opponent's shin if you're grabbed from behind or in his ribs or face if you're both on the ground. Drive your heel into your target area.

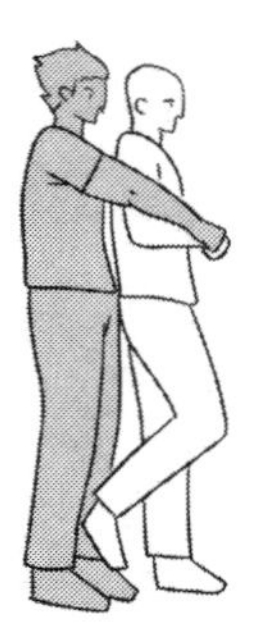

Side Kick

The side kick can be aimed in any direction, and if you add the skip it can be very powerful and useful to cover distance.

If your opponent is close, raise your leg and snap your heel into your target, such as his knee or shin. Retract it quickly.

If using the skip, spring forward with your rear leg, allowing your rear foot to replace your lead foot as it springs up into kicking position and simultaneously travels toward your target.

As your back foot replaces your front, straighten your lead leg and kick into your target.

Rear/Side Headbutt

Slam the back of your head into your target.

ESCAPING CHOKES

Protecting your airway is paramount.

Grab your opponent's arm with both your hands and jerk down as hard as you can, so you can tuck your chin down and towards his elbow.

From here, work to loosen his grip and attack any way you can. Bite, bend his fingers, kick, attack his groin, etc.

Remember, if he is attacking you from behind, then you need to face and attack.

Tucking your chin is a good way to prevent him choking you.

FIGHTING MULTIPLE OPPONENTS

In the following section titles, the first number is your "team." For example, "two vs. one" means two of you against one opponent. Communication between teammates is needed to adapt to the situation—if one of you is in trouble, to finish effectively, etc.

Two vs. One

Advance together on either side of the enemy. As you close in, whichever one of you he isn't focused on should go for his legs while the other concentrates on his upper body.

Three vs. Two

Advance and close, so that the two of you on the outside are on either side of your enemies. Whoever is facing his opponent alone can fight or stall until the other two have finished and can come to his aid.

Even Numbers

One fighter stays in reserve until the enemy has committed their entire force. The reserved fighter then attacks from behind.

One vs. Two or More

Stay on your feet and use your surroundings to create a situation where you are only facing one opponent at a time. Put them in each other's way if you can.

If you end up on the ground (avoid this at all costs) move into a corner or against a wall. Use a modified guard in which your legs are not exposed.

Two vs. Three

Both of you attack one opponent at a time until you have defeated all three. If you are separated, then fighter 1 defends against two, while fighter 2 fights one on one. Fighter 2 comes to fighter 1's aid when he has finished with his opponent.

STAND-UP FIGHTING STRATEGIC GUIDE

Get a weapon

If you can, attack your opponent from behind, either:

- with a rear naked choke; or
- by striking the base of his skull.

If you have him face-on, strike first and knock him out.

If your initial strikes don't KO him, either:

- choke him out using the RNC or guillotine; or
- put him on the ground.

If he strikes first:

- burst;
- slip, parry, and strike;
- cover and rush; or
- sprawl and guillotine.

If your initial rush doesn't stop him, fight on until there is an opportunity to rush.

If you become overwhelmed:

- Cover up and attack when possible.
- Bear-hug him.
- Headbutt him or attack his eyes or groin.

If you are grabbed by surprise:

- Twist and/or jerk.

- Hit his forearm mound.
- Attack his hands/fingers.

If you are attacked from the rear or side:

- Escape his grip.
- Face and attack him.

To escape a choke hold:

- Protect your airway.
- Tuck your chin toward his elbow.
- Attack him.
- Loosen his grip.
- Escape.

If you're thrown to the ground, either:

- roll or break fall, then get up; or
- cover up, then bring him down.

MULTIPLE OPPONENTS STRATEGIC GUIDE

Two vs. One

- Advance from the sides at the same time.
- One of you should attack your opponent's upper body, while the other attacks his lower body.

Three vs. Two

- Advance so two of you are on either side of the enemy.
- One must fight alone until the others can help.

Even Numbers

- Keep one fighter in reserve until the enemy commits their entire force.
- Have your reserve fighter attack from behind.

One vs. Two or More

- Escape, if possible.
- Get a weapon.
- Line up your opponents.
- Stay off the ground.

Two vs. Three

- Both attack one opponent at a time.

GROUND FIGHTING

In a street fight, it is preferable to stay on your feet, but knowing how to ground fight is a very important skill to have.

Many street fights will end up on the ground, whether you want them to or not. If you are up against a very skilled stand-up fighter, you may also decide to bring the fight to the ground so you have a better chance of winning.

CONSERVE YOUR ENERGY

A ground fight may last a while, and if it drags on, the winner will be the one with the most endurance.

Take your time and observe your opponent. Let him wear out.

Avoid using brute strength. Instead, feel his body and use his movements to your advantage.

If you find yourself in a position where you are tied up, don't waste energy struggling. Get your legs free first, then your arms.

THE GROUND POSITION

When your opponent manages to get you on the ground while he is still standing, adopt the ground position. As soon as you hit the ground, swing your feet to face your attacker. Use one arm to defend yourself and one leg to kick at your opponent's knees if he comes towards you. Use your other hand and foot to scoot yourself away from him until you have enough distance to get up.

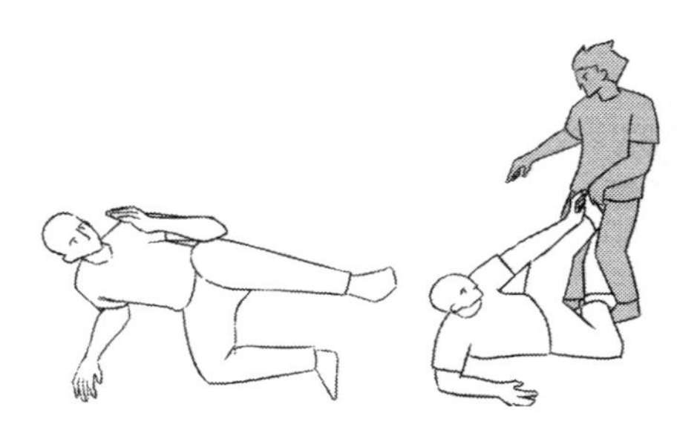

Getting Back on Your Feet

When the timing is right, swing your feet behind you so that they are close to the fighter's position. Use one hand to push yourself up off the ground, and the other to protect your face. Stand up and adopt the FP.

Note: While you are on the ground, if possible, pick up a weapon, such as dirt to throw in your opponent's eyes. You can also do this if rolling.

BRINGING YOUR OPPONENT DOWN TO THE GROUND

There may be a time where you are on the ground and your opponent is attacking you while still on his feet. You will need to bring him down.

Cover Up on the Ground

If your opponent's attack is too aggressive and you are unable to get up, you will need to cover up to protect yourself.

Use the outer side of your forearms to protect your head. Rest or press your palms on your ears or forehead, and stick your elbows out in front of you. If you can, hold your forearms towards the direction of attack. Keep your eyes up, your chin tucked, and your teeth together. Tuck your knees up. If possible, keep your heels pressed against your bum. Stay on your back.

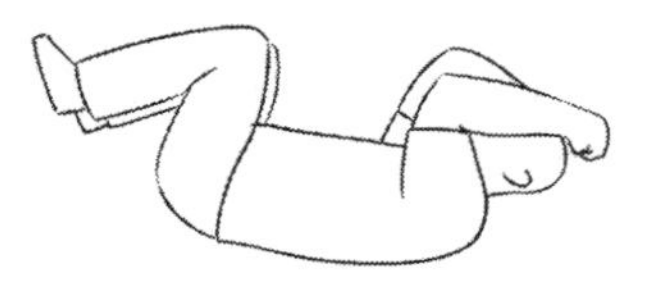

Then Bring Your Opponent to the Ground

As a kick comes in, or when he gets close enough, grab his leg (preferably both) and hug it/them tight at his knee(s). Lean all your weight at a downward diagonal angle at his thighs to bring him to the ground.

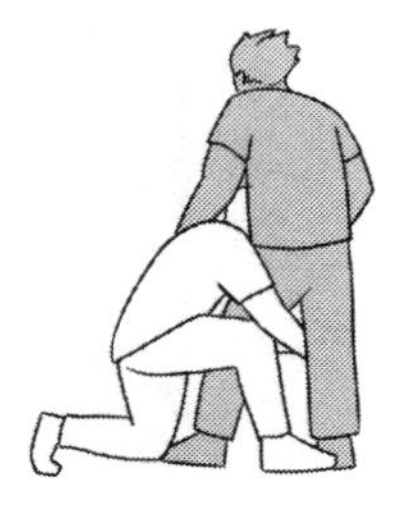

THE BEST POSITION: THE BACK MOUNT

The back mount (a.k.a. rear mount) is the very best position you can be in during a ground fight.

Adopting the Back Mount

Sit on your opponent's back, facing the same way. Wrap both legs around him, with your heels hooked inside his legs. Never cross your feet. Once you are stable, apply the rear naked choke.

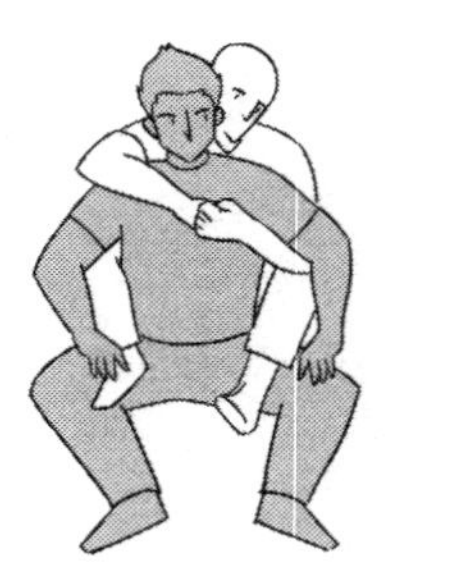
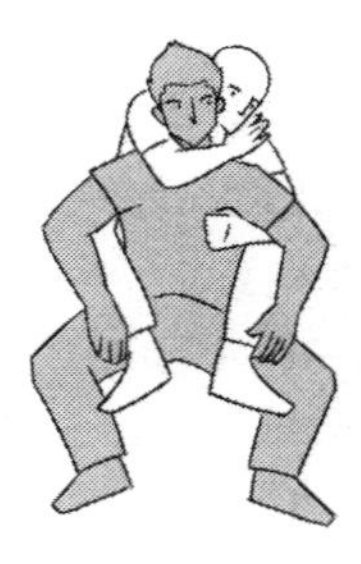
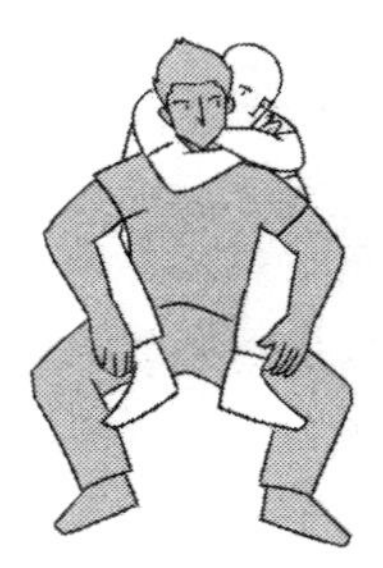

Escaping the Back Mount

If you are caught in the back mount, immediately place one arm beside your ear and the other across your body, angled into your armpit. This prevents the RNC. Position yourself so that your opponent is underneath you—that is, so you are both facing the sky.

Fall on the side towards your raised arm and push yourself up to scrape out of the back mount. Get on your feet.

Related Chapter:

- Rear Naked Choke

THE NEXT BEST POSITION: THE FULL MOUNT

If you cannot achieve the back mount, adopt the full mount.

Sit on your opponent's torso so that you are facing him. Get your knees as far up toward his armpits as possible.

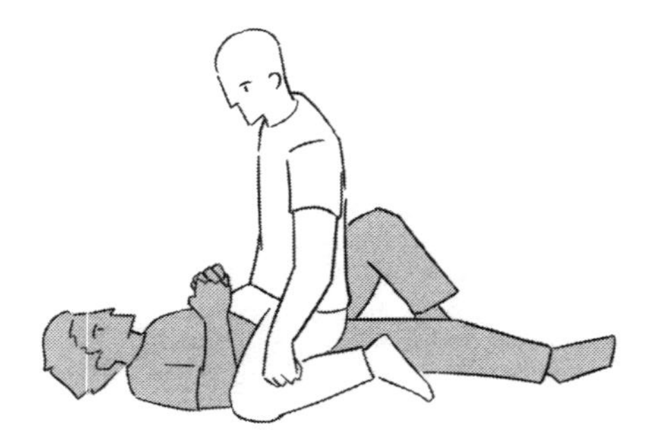

To Prevent Your Opponent From Escaping

Squeeze his midsection with your thighs, put your feet underneath his hips to control them. Holding his head will also limit his movements.

When he does try to escape, use your arms, elbows, and head to stabilize yourself.

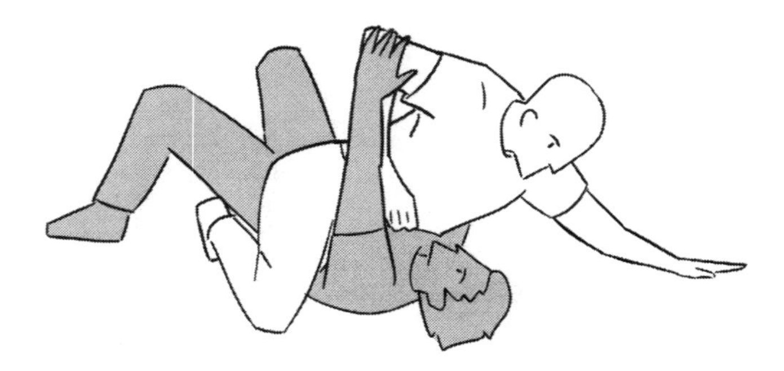

Full Mount to Back Mount

If you have the full mount, your initial goal is to get into the best position, the rear mount.

Strike Your Opponent's Face

Ensure you do not lose your balance or hit the ground.

When he turns to protect himself, let him. Once you are on his back, apply the RNC.

If He Does Not Roll Over, Force Him

If he protects himself from strikes with his arms, use both of your hands to push his arm across his body, and then lean on him to capture it.

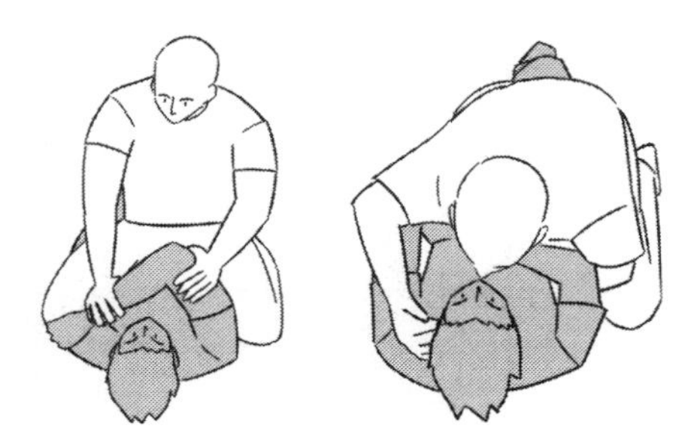

Reach around his head and grab the wrist of the captured hand.

Place your free hand on his elbow to hold him in place, and then reposition yourself so that you can use your chest to force him over.

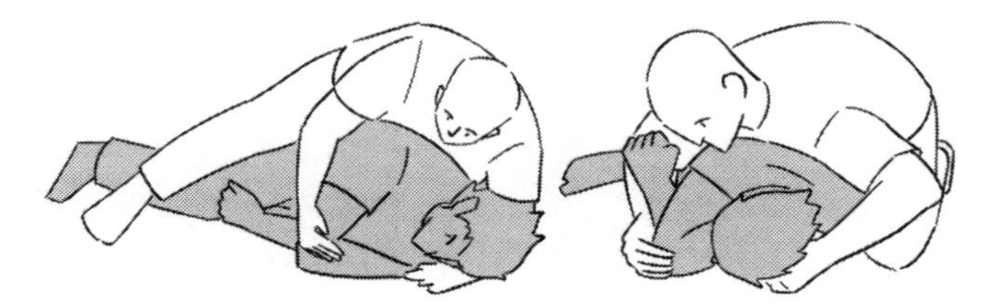

Chokes From the Full Mount

Choke 1

Lean your forearm onto your opponent's throat and put your weight into it. To increase leverage, place your other arm behind his neck.

Grab the bicep or forearm of the arm that is on his throat. Use the hand of that arm to grab your other arm.

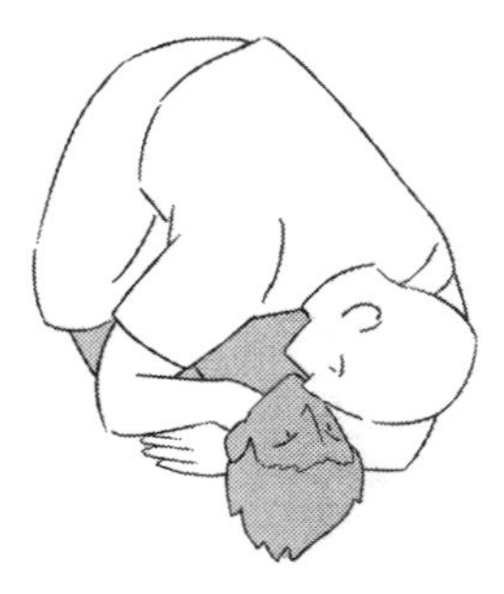

Choke 2

Place your fists on either side of your opponent's Adam's apple, with your pinkies acting as the base.

Drive the knuckles of both your pointer fingers into his neck on either side of his Adam's apple.

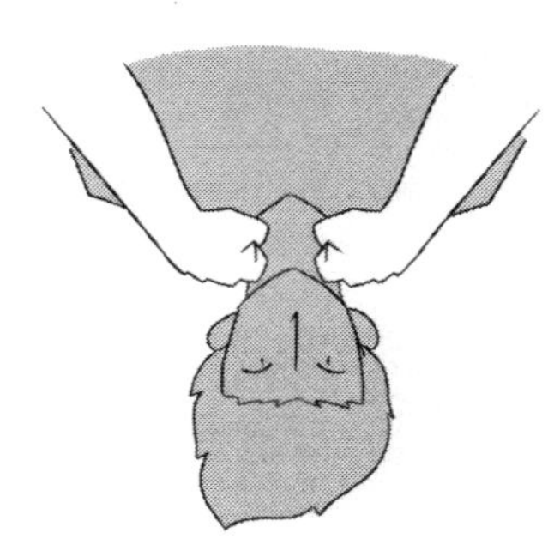

Choke 3

Place your right arm behind/under your opponent's head. Grab your left wrist with your right hand. Use your right shoulder and left fist to press on his arteries.

Escaping the Full Mount

Escaping the Full Mount 1

Twist your opponent's head, pull his hair, attack his groin, and buck to get him off.

If that doesn't work, use the trap and roll. The principle is to isolate one side of your opponent so you can roll him over that side.

Secure one of his arms and place your foot over his leg/ankle/foot on that same side. Keep your elbows tucked in as much as possible.

Jerk your hips up and continue rolling over to his isolated side until you are on top of him. Strike him.

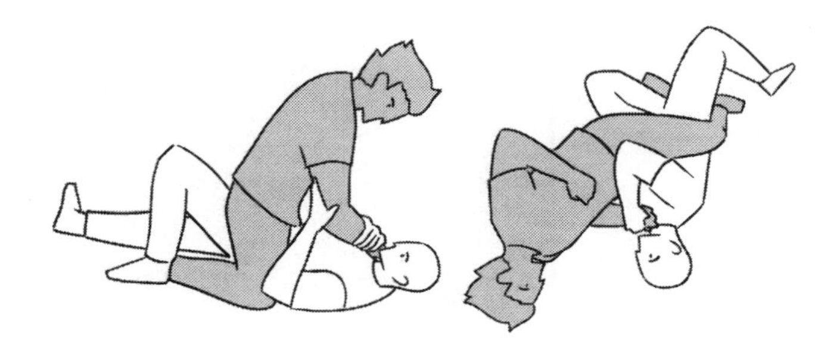

Escaping the Full Mount 2

If you cannot use the trap and roll, use the elbow escape. Be careful, because you will be lowering your guard.

At the end of this move, you will still be underneath your opponent, but you will have him in your guard.

Turn on your side, with your leg flat on the ground. Hold your opponent's leg in place and bring your knee through the opening.

Once your knee is past his leg, put your weight on the same leg.

Turn towards the other side so you can pull your leg out and wrap it around his back.

Repeat the movement on the other side.

Put him in your guard.

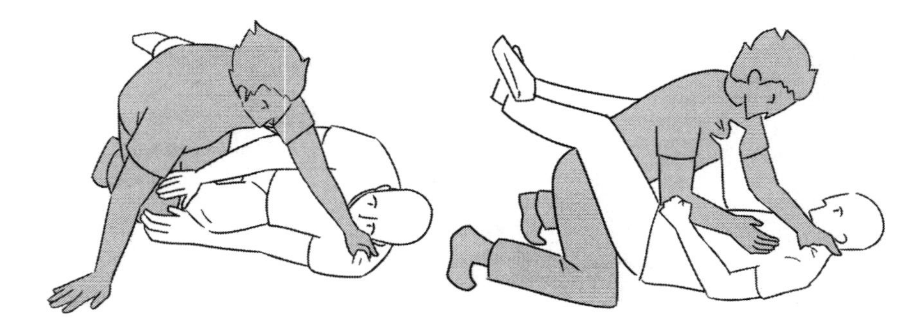

Cross your ankles tightly and stick close to your opponent to prevent being struck.

Apply the guillotine.

Once you have him locked in, push him away with your legs while pulling his neck towards your chin.

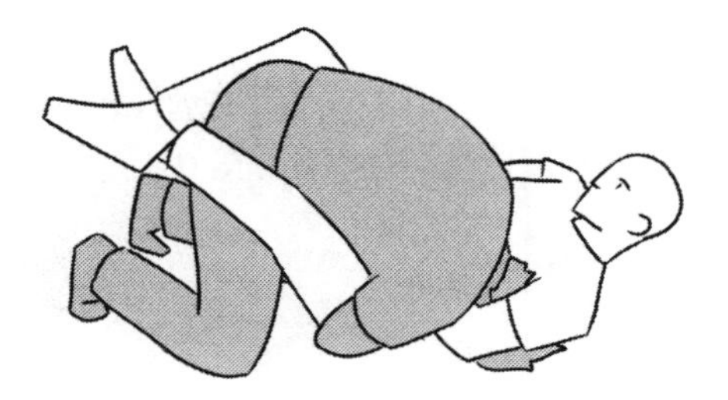

Related Chapters:

- Rear Naked Choke
- Guillotine Choke
- The Best Position: The Back Mount

THE STRAIGHT ARM BAR

If you have your opponent in the full mount and he tries to push you off/twist your head, etc., you can apply the straight-arm bar.

If you want his right arm, place your right hand on your opponent's chest, in between his arms. This will isolate that arm.

Wrap your left arm around the outside of his right arm and place it on your right hand.

Lean your weight on your opponent's chest and swing your left foot around the top of his head.

Sit down as close to his shoulder as you can.

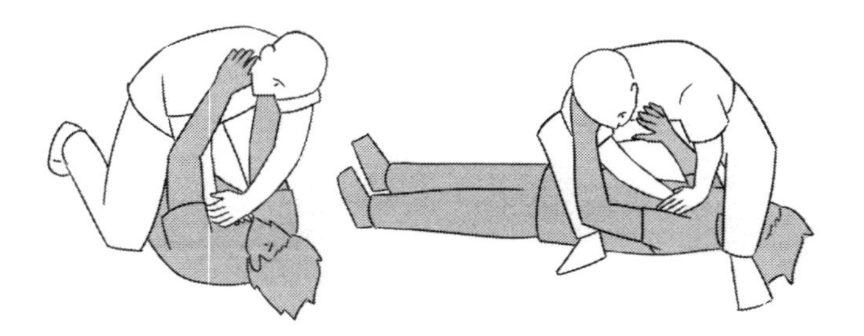

Grip his arm so his thumb is pointing up, and lie back.

Cross your ankles and squeeze your knees to clasp his arm. Lie back. Raise your hips and pull back on his arm.

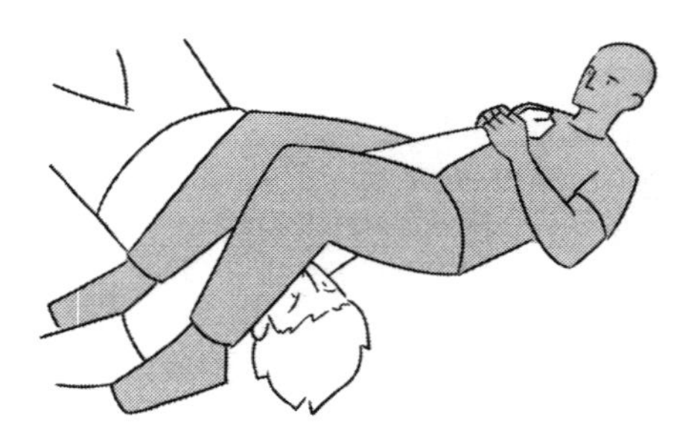

Escaping/Preventing the Straight Arm Bar

Do everything you can to bring your hands together in monkey grip.

Push your opponent's leg off your face.

Use your legs to drive your body back until his leg is pinned to the ground by your head.

With your hands still together, spin toward your opponent until you are in his guard.

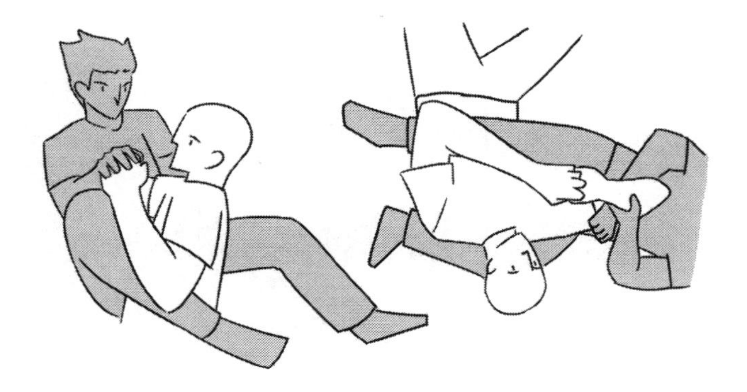

If You Cannot Do Monkey Grip

Twist your thumb sideways, toward your head.

Create distance by getting your hips off the floor and moving your feet as far away from your opponent's head as you can.

Roll backwards until your chest is close to the ground, and bring your knees under your body. Jerk your arm out.

Related Chapter:

- The Next Best Position: The Full Mount

IF YOUR OPPONENT PUTS YOU IN HIS GUARD

When you use the trap and roll, you will probably end up in your opponent's guard. This means that his back will be on the ground with you on top of him, but his legs will be free, as opposed to when you are in the full mount, where his legs are behind you.

Strike him.

If necessary/possible, move over his legs into the mount.

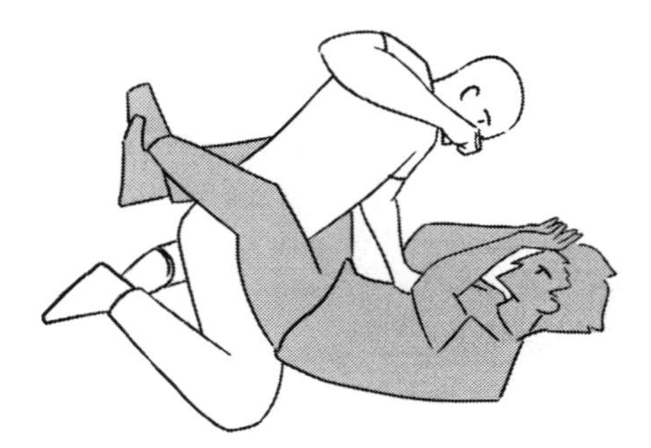

If Your Opponent Has His Legs Crossed and Pulls You In

Swim your arms to the inside of his, then sit back and keep him down, with your hands on his torso.

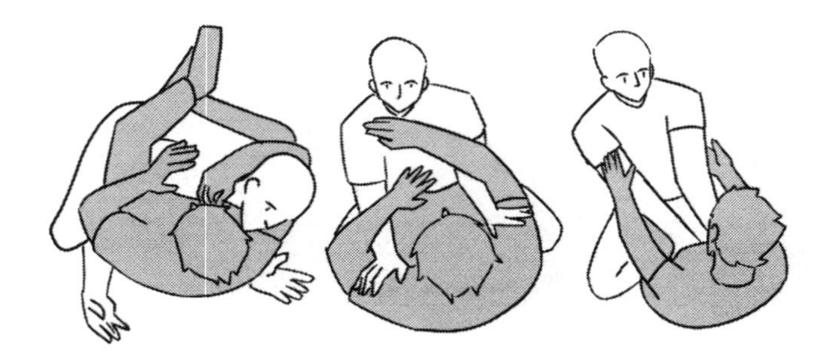

Strike him until he uncrosses his legs, and then hook your elbows under his knees.

Dip one shoulder underneath his knee and cup his shoulder with that hand.

Your other hand should hold his thigh.

Push forward with your feet to “stack” him.

Keep a wide base for balance and turn your head in case he tries to strike you.

“Walk” around to the side, keeping your wide base.

Lift your head to get around his leg while you drop your chest onto him to adopt side control.

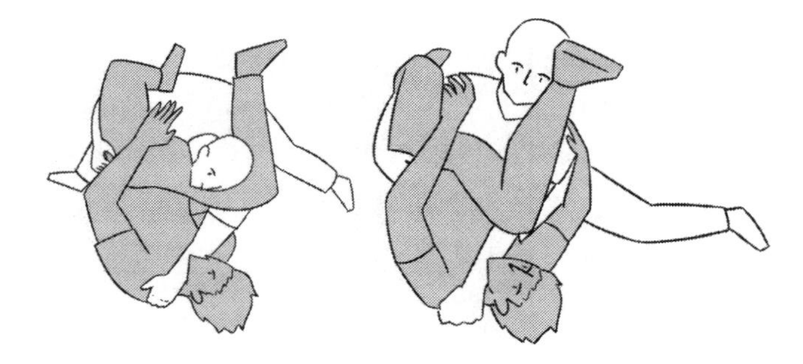

Related Chapter:

- The Next Best Position: The Full Mount

ATTACKS FROM THE GUARD

If you end up on the bottom in a ground fight, putting your opponent in the guard position is the best thing to do. Cross your legs around his waist and use your hips to control his distance.

In most cases, you will want to pull him in close to prevent him from striking you. Doing so will also allow you to attack.

Chokes From the Guard

You can easily adapt a number of chokes from the guard position. The guillotine choke is especially good.

As you apply it with your arms, use your legs to pull your opponent's torso away. This will make the chokehold more effective.

Choke 3 from the full mount is also good to use.

Straight Arm Bar From the Guard

If you cannot apply a choke, try the straight arm bar. Capture your opponent's arms to prevent him from striking you.

Release your legs, spin and place them over his head, capturing the target arm between them. You can use your hand on his leg to help you spin. Extend your body to apply the arm bar.

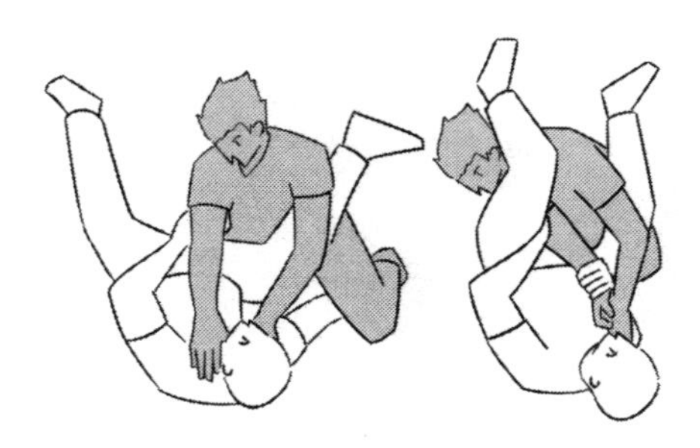

Related Chapters:

- Guillotine Choke
- The Next Best Position: The Full Mount
- The Straight Arm Bar
- If Your Opponent Puts You in His Guard

SIDE CONTROL

Lie perpendicularly over your opponent, who is facing up. Put your elbow on the ground in the notch created by his head and shoulder.

Your other hand should be palm-down on the ground on the near side of your opponent. The leg closest to his head should be straight, and the other one bent against his hip.

Keep your head down to avoid knee strikes.

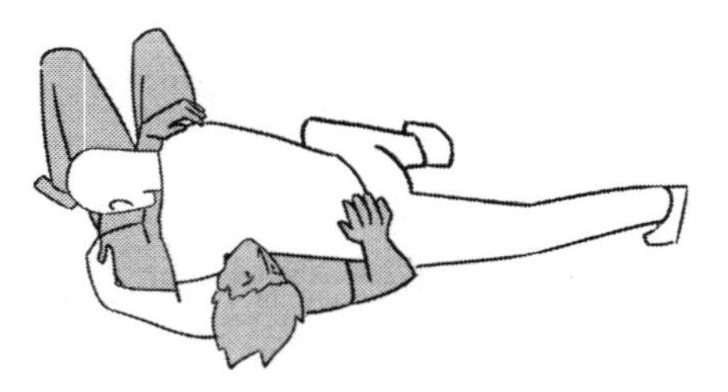

Side Control to the Full or Rear Mount

Bring your knees up close under your opponent's armpit and put your elbow in his neck. Do knee strikes with the leg closest to his legs.

If he turns away, take his back. If he turns towards you, adopt the full mount.

Attacks From Side Control

If you can't get into the mount position, attack from side control.

Put your knee somewhere on his torso, like his stomach or chest.

Extend your other leg for balance.

From here, you can strike, apply an arm bar, or get up.

Related Chapters

- The Best Position: The Back Mount
- The Next Best Position: The Full Mount

ESCAPING THE CLASSIC HEADLOCK

People who do not know how to ground fight will often apply the common headlock.

Grab and twist your opponent's genitals or twist his head to escape.

If that is not possible, turn on your side to face him. Bring your top arm under his jawbone and hold your wrist with your other hand to form a frame. Rotate so that you are on your knees at his back.

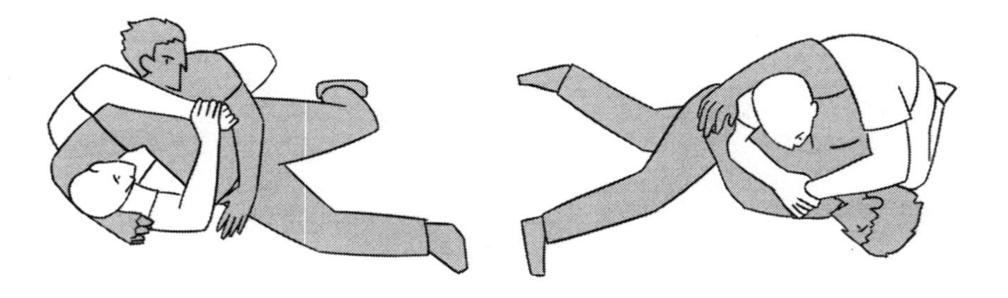

If you want, you can step over him. Apply pressure with your frame until he lets go.

THE ONLY LEG LOCK YOU NEED TO KNOW

Although your goal should not be to apply a leg lock, they are good to know in case the opportunity presents itself.

There are many types of legs locks, but this one (the heel hook) is easy to apply and very effective.

Be very careful in training. Damage is often done before it is felt.

To perform this move, put both your legs around one of your opponent's. Place his instep against your ribs and hook his heel in your wrist.

Immobilize his upper leg and hips with your legs. Turn your upper body to rotate his lower leg. Either his pinkie or his big toe will be on top.

This move can also be done when he is on his stomach.

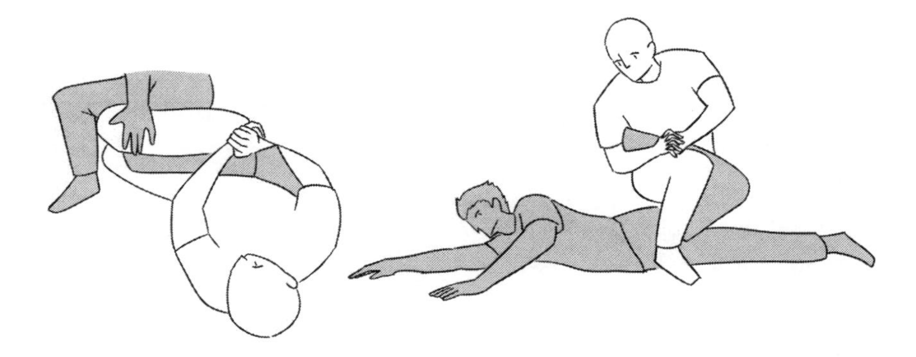

Related Chapter:

- Training Methods

GROUND FIGHTING STRATEGIC GUIDE

Offensive

Perform a back mount, and apply the RNC. If you can't do a back mount, perform a full mount.

From the full mount, do one of the following (in order of preference):

- Perform a back mount.
- Choke your opponent from the front.
- Apply the straight arm bar.

If you are in your opponent's guard, gain side control, then (in order of preference):

- Perform a rear mount.
- Achieve a full mount.
- Attack from side control.

If you have him in your guard, apply one of the following (in order of preference):

- Guillotine
- Straight arm bar

If the opportunity arises, apply a leg lock.

Defensive

No matter what position you are in, the defensive strategy is the same.

Defend against attacks.

Achieve one of the following offensive positions (in order of preference):

- Rear mount
- Full mount
- Side control
- Guard

Use the most appropriate offensive strategy.

WEAPONRY

Using a weapon will give you a great advantage, but you must consider use of force in comparison to the situation. Actually, you should always consider use of force, but even more so when weapons are involved.

HOW ANYTHING CAN BE USED AS A WEAPON

There are five categories of objects that can be used as weapons. Train with objects that you commonly have access to, such as the tools of your trade or the baseball bat you keep beside your bed.

Close-Range

This category includes items that are generally used with one hand, like a knife, bottle, comb, pair of scissors, pen, or rolled-up magazine.

Hold the item back close to your waist and thrust it at your opponent's face and/or lower torso.

Mid-Range

This category includes items that can be held with one or two hands depending on their length, weight, range, etc. Some examples are a chair leg, rubber hose, metal pipe, broomstick, baseball bat, or walking stick.

Swing your weapon from different angles at your opponent's knees, ribs, head and the top of his shoulder. Thrust it at his face and lower torso.

Pliable

This category includes any loosely pliable object, such as a skipping rope, telephone cord, or piece of clothing.

Depending on the material, it may be used to tangle your opponent in and/or to strike him with. It is best at about 1 meter in length. Fold or gather it to adjust its length.

Projectiles

This category includes military-type weapons like guns, grenades, and mines, etc. as well as non-military and improvised projectiles and sprays, such as ashtrays, deodorant, hot liquid, or dirt.

Shields

This category includes anything you can hide behind to defend yourself or any stationary object you can ram someone into, such as a chair, door, wall, or bin lid.

Related Chapters:

- Close-Range Weapons
- Mid-Range Weapons
- Pliable Weapons
- Projectiles
- Shields

GENERAL GRIP AND STANCE

General Grip

When gripping a weapon, hold it tightly enough so that your opponent cannot take it from your hand, but not so tightly it causes fatigue. Use your whole hand to grip it, including your thumb. It should be held inside your fist.

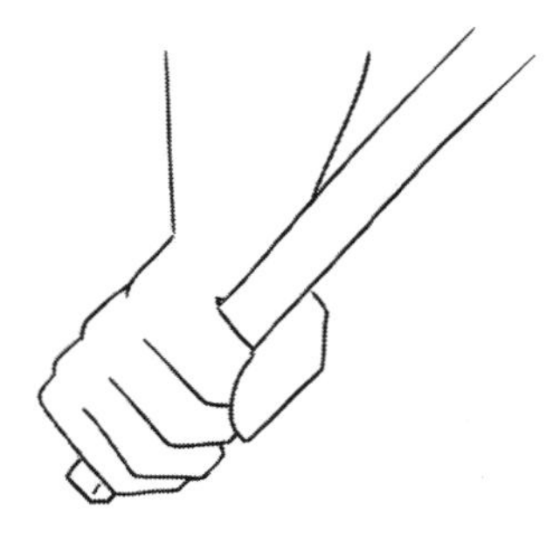

General Stance

If holding a weapon in one hand, stand in the fighter's position, but with your weak side as lead.

The weapon should be held in your strong hand, in the rear. This will make it harder for your opponent to grab your weapon, while still letting you get maximum power out if it. Keep your lead hand up to guard your head and torso if needed.

If holding a weapon with two hands, stand in the fighter's position, with your strong side as lead.

The position of your hands will depend on the length/weight of the weapon and your personal preference. The further apart your hands are, the stronger and faster your strikes can be, but you will lose range.

SINGLE STRIKES

Every weapon can make strikes from any angle in forward and reverse. The following are basic angles of attack to be built upon.

Swing the weapon smoothly. Be aggressive, but let the weight of the weapon drive through the target, then either strike again or return to your ready position. Some strikes are better suited to certain weapons and target areas.

Downward

From your ready position, swing down in a slightly diagonal motion across your body and through your target, and then return to your ready position or go into another strike. Aim for your opponent's knee, collarbone, or head.

Horizontal

Start from the ready position and swing into your target horizontally from the side. This can also be done in reverse by starting where your first strike would have finished if you had missed. Aim for your opponent's ribs.

Upward

Start from where a downward strike would end and swing up into and through your target. Aim for your opponent's groin, ribs, or head.

Thrust

Drive the tip of your weapon into your target. Aim for your opponent's lower torso (stomach and ribs) and face.

Central

This strike is useful if your opponent is too close for you to use other strikes effectively.

Hold the weapon evenly spread in both hands and drive the center of it into his face or throat.

CLOSE-RANGE WEAPONS

Thrust attacks are your go-to with close-range weapons.

1 – 2

The 1-2 combination can be used in the same way as you normally would. Strike first with your lead to distract your opponent, and then follow up with a thrust.

3-Step

Feint a strike with your knife. When your opponent goes to combat it, quickly follow up with the 1-2.

Spin Attack

Start with the 1-2, then grab your opponent's arm, spin him to expose his back and stab him repeatedly in the kidneys.

Note: This will probably kill him if you are using a sharp object.

MID-RANGE WEAPONS

One-Handed

The bottom of the weapon should extend between one and two inches below your little finger.

Most of the strikes should come from behind your head, as this will give you the greatest power. To enable this, stand with the object held near your ear in your strong hand. The tip of the weapon should face your back.

Your empty lead hand should be held open and vertically, close to your center line. This is your ready position.

If you have two short-range weapons, and you can hold each with one hand, then hold the second across your body.

Your strike rate will be much faster (with practice), and you can parry with one and strike with the other.

Two-Handed

The further apart your hands are, the stronger and faster your strikes will be, but you will sacrifice distance.

If your hands are close together, hold your weapon like you would a baseball bat. Hold it vertically and on a 45° angle in front of your body.

Your lead hand should be above your rear, and because you are using a two-handed weapon, your strong side should be your lead.

If your hands are further apart, then hold the weapon diagonally across your body, with your hands facing opposite directions.

Sliding

Short-range weapons that are long enough can be slid within your grip, which will allow you to switch between short- and long-range techniques. Doing so is useful for combinations and the parry and strike.

For example, to do two downward strikes, hold the weapon with your hands wide apart.

As you strike, loosen the grip of your top hand. Just before you make contact, or when your hands are close together, tighten your grip. After you make contact, loosen the grip of that hand again and draw the weapon back.

Tighten your grip and loosen the grip of your other hand to do another downward strike with the other end of the weapon.

Related Chapter:

- Attack Combinations

PLIABLE WEAPONS

A pliable weapon can be used to strike or tangle your opponent.

Grip it with your pinkie, ring, and middle fingers. Your thumb and index finger will then be free to reinforce the grip or hold the weapon gathered in a wad or loop, depending on how big it is.

Upward strikes are best. Be careful not to hit your opponent's weapon, or yours will wrap around it.

Thrusting is best done at the face, and can be done by whipping/flicking your weapon like you would a towel.

Tangle Method

The tangle method can be used "tie your opponent up," and is effective for applying chokes.

If your pliable object is too light, you may be forced to use the tangle method for it to be effective.

Hold the weapon with both hands, about shoulder-width apart but so there is some slack in the line. Do not wrap it around your hand, but grip it firmly.

Capturing the leg of a kicker is not practical, so go for his neck. Never try to capture his arm if he is wielding a blade.

If you capture his arm, it is a good “stepping stone” to going for his neck. Even if you cannot choke him out, it is the basis for “tying him up,” which will enable you to lead into other attacks.

To choke him out, keep one of your hands at the base of his neck while pulling up with the other.

PROJECTILES

There are two types of projectiles; mechanical and improvised.

Most military-type weapons, (guns, explosives, etc.) and primitive weapons (bow and arrow, spear, blowgun, etc.) make up the mechanical projectiles. Improvised projectiles are the everyday objects you can throw at your opponent. They can be liquids, sand, stones, ashtrays, etc.

Improvised Weapons

Most improvised projectiles are used best to create a distraction. You can throw a rock at something to create a noise and focus your opponent's attention, or go for his eyes/face.

Never throw something that could be used more effectively if held in your hand.

Throwing

Start with your weak side forward and the object in your strong hand. Face and look at your target. Rock back a little bit and turn your body so your lead shoulder points at your target.

In a continuous motion, raise your hands up to your chest.

Bring your lead leg around and lift your knee up to approximately waist level (or higher, if it's more comfortable). Keep your back straight and your body compact.

Point your lead hand and elbow towards the target. In this position, your arms and torso should form a T.

Bring your front leg down and point your foot towards the target. Push off the ground with your back leg.

As you land with your front toe pointed forward, bring your throwing elbow up over your shoulder, and drive your lead hand and elbow back into your hip.

Next, rotate your torso toward the target and release the object. All your body's momentum will drive it forward.

As you release the object, snap your wrist downward. After the object leaves your hand, continue your motion by bringing your throwing arm all the way down to your opposite knee.

Mechanical Weapons

In most countries, a civilian will not come across mechanical projectiles, especially of the military kind.

You need only familiarize yourself with the rifle, shotgun, and handgun.

The best place to do this is a shooting range. You will get safety lessons, learn how to operate the weapon, and probably learn how to shoot accurately as well.

Shooting Straight

The following are general guidelines for shooting straight. They apply to most military firearms as well as to primitive mechanical projectiles like the bow and arrow, crossbow, etc.

Aim for your opponent's upper torso.

Grip on your weapon firmly enough to support the weapon as well as recoil. Your hold should be firm. Gripping too tightly will decrease your accuracy.

Your positioning should be balanced. Generally, the lower you are to the ground, the better. Lying on your stomach is the preferable position.

Position yourself in such a way that your weapon naturally points in the direction of your target.

Take a deep breath to calm your mind and body. Take more if needed, but not so many as to get light-headed.

When you're ready to shoot, exhale completely. When your lungs are entirely empty, hold your breath, take aim at your target, and take the shot.

If you are using a gun, the trigger must be squeezed calmly and completely depressed. Pause just a moment before releasing the trigger. This squeezing method prevents you from jerking the firearm when you shoot.

SHIELDS

Shields are held with two hands and used to block or strike. Immovable objects, like walls, can be used by ramming your opponent's head into them.

IF YOU BOTH HAVE WEAPONS

Apart from all the normal target areas, you can strike your opponent's hand so he drops his weapon.

If Your Opponent's Weapon is Longer Than Yours

Bridge the gap so you can attack. This can be done with good timing and footwork or with the parry and strike.

As the strike comes in, move towards it and parry it to the side as you move out of the path, preferably towards your opponent, then counter.

When you parry a longer weapon with a shorter one, you will most likely need to reinforce your parry with your hand, as well as to maneuver out of the way. Use a flat hand behind your weapon to ensure that you do not get hit.

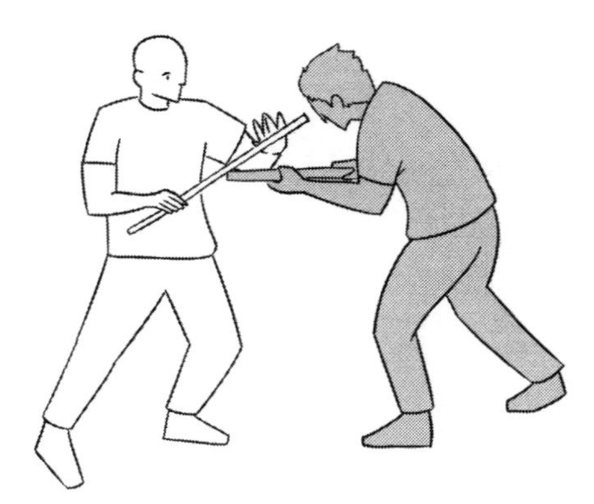

If You Hold the Longer Weapon

Keep your range advantage. Thrusts will be harder for your opponent to move in on.

IF YOUR OPPONENT HAS A WEAPON AND YOU DON'T

If it is an option, comply with your opponent's demands.

If the attack is immediate and you have no room/time to move out of the way, burst at him as he strikes.

If you do have room to move, then maintain a distance of at least 10 feet plus the length of his weapon.

Try to place stationary objects between yourself and your attacker and find weapon of your own.

If You Cannot Get a Weapon

When your opponent strikes, move out of the line of attack and/or redirect the weapon away from you.

Secure the weapon and/or the limb holding the weapon. Attack him hard and disarm him with a bite, arm lock, etc.

Arm Locks for Disarming and Compliance

Arm locks can be used to gain compliance and/or to disarm someone.

Manipulate your opponent's arm/shoulder/wrist joint(s) up to and beyond its/their extreme range of motion.

The way in which you do it depends on the situation, the type of weapon, your position etc.

Shown below are a number of arm locks that can be modified if needed.

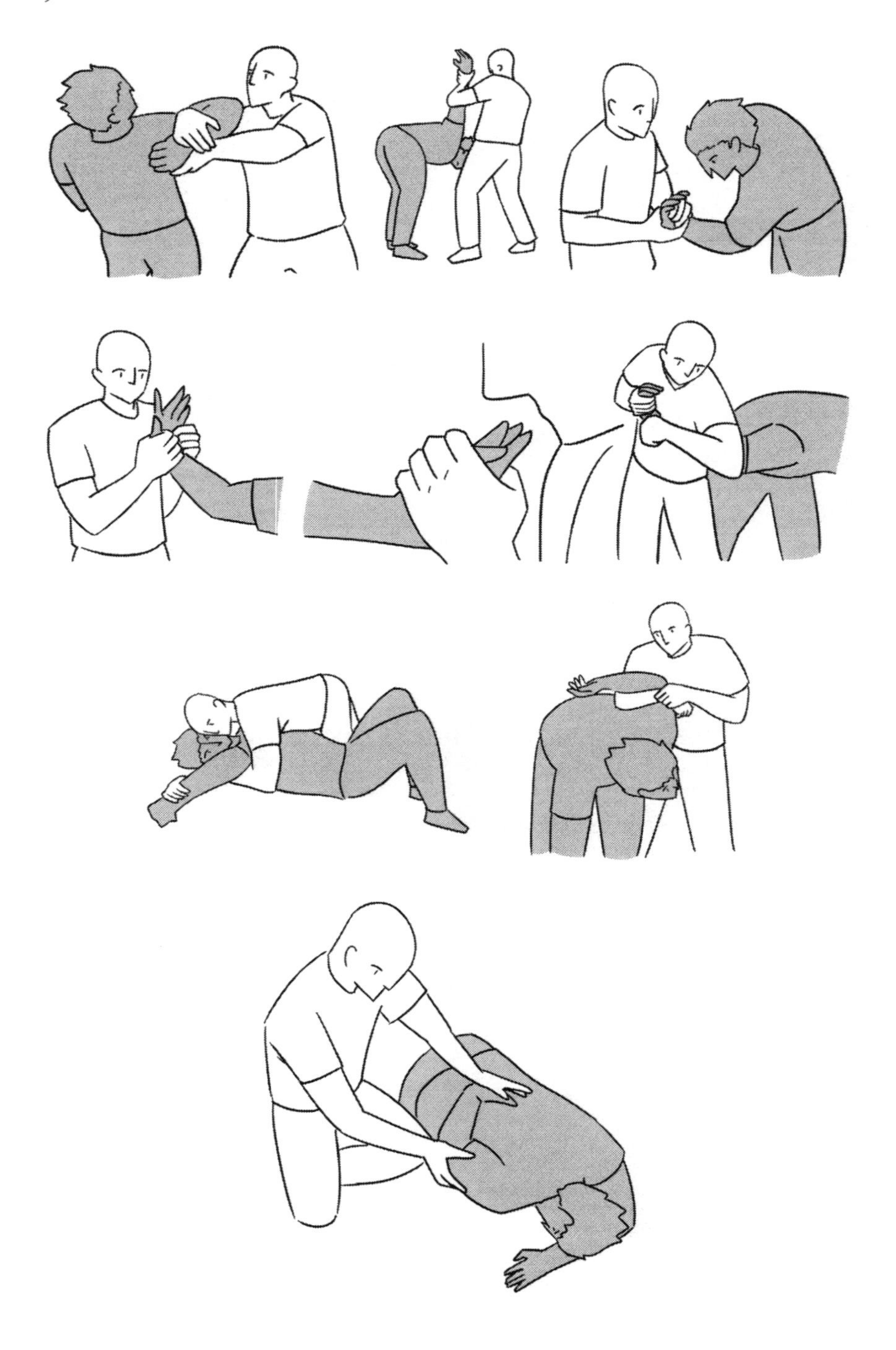

Defense Against Guns

The action you decide to take when faced with a gun (compliance, running away, disarming, etc.) will depend on you and the situation.

Usually it is best to comply, especially if the demands are purely materialistic—if you are being robbed at gunpoint, for example.

It is difficult to aim accurately with a handgun if the target is more than 10 meters away, especially if that target is moving erratically. If your opponent has a shotgun or rifle, then his ability to accurately shoot increases.

If you decide to run, be erratic in your movement (roll, zigzag, etc.)

If you are within arm's reach, grab hold of your opponent's weapon while staying out of the line of fire, and twist it away from you and toward him.

Related Chapter:

- If Your Opponent Strikes First

WEAPONRY STRATEGIC GUIDE

If your opponent has a weapon and you don't:

- Comply.
- Find a weapon.
- Escape.
- Disarm him.

If you both have weapons and:

You have the longer one, then keep your range advantage.

You have the shorter weapon, bridge the gap and attack.

THANKS FOR READING

Dear reader,

Thank you for reading *How To Street Fight.*

If you enjoyed this book, please leave a review where you bought it. It helps more than most people think.

Don't forget your FREE book chapters!

You will also be among the first to know of FREE review copies, discount offers, bonus content, and more.

Go to:

https://offers.SFNonfictionBooks.com/Free-Chapters

Thanks again for your support.

REFERENCES

AppOpus. (2012). *U.S. Army Field Manual FM 3-25.150 (21-150) COMBATIVES: Expanded Edition*. AppOpus.

Cheung, W. (1852). *Dynamic Chi Sao by William Cheung.* Unique Publications.

DeMile, J. (1977). *Tao of Wing Chun Do, Vol. 2: Bruce Lee's Chi Sao*. Tao of Wing Chun Do.

Filotto, G. (2011). *Systema : The Russian Martial System.* CreateSpace Independent Publishing Platform.

Gracie, C. (2003). *Cesar Gracie Brazilian Jiu-Jitsu & Gracie Jiu-Jitsu Grappling Instructional Series.* Ultimate Imports.

Gutierrez, V. (2009). *WingTsun. Chi Sao II.* Sportimex.

Indio, D. (2012). *Mixed Martial Arts Fighting Techniques: Apply Modern Training Methods Used by MMA Pros!.* Tuttle Publishing.

Jacques, M. (2009). *The Grappler's Handbook Gi and No-Gi Techniques.* Black Belt Books.

Kemerly, T. Snyder, S. (2009) *Taekwondo Grappling Techniques: Hone Your Competitive Edge for Mixed Martial Arts.* Tuttle Publishing.

Lee, B. (2008). *Bruce Lee's Fighting Method.* Black Belt Communications.

Lee, B. (2011). *Tao of Jeet Kune Do: Expanded Edition.* Black Belt Communications.

Lung, Haha. Prowant, C. (2000). *Ninja Shadowhand - The Art Of Invisibility*. Citadel Press.

Mamiko, V. (2012). *Systema No Contact Combat.* Varangian Press.

Plyler, D. Seibert, C. (2009) *The Ultimate Mixed Martial Arts Training Guide: Techniques for Fitness, Self Defense, and Competition.* Krause Publications.

Yeo, S. (2011). *Ninjutsu: The Secret Art of the Ninja*. Crowood.

Yimm Lee, J. (1972). *Wing Chun Kung-Fu.* Ohara Publications.

AUTHOR RECOMMENDATIONS

Teach Yourself Self-Defense

This is the only self-defense training manual you need, because these are the best street fighting moves around.

Get it now.

www.SFNonfictionBooks.com/Self-Defense-Handbook

ABOUT SAM FURY

Sam Fury has had a passion for survival, evasion, resistance, and escape (SERE) training since he was a young boy growing up in Australia.

This led him to years of training and career experience in related subjects, including martial arts, military training, survival skills, outdoor sports, and sustainable living.

These days, Sam spends his time refining existing skills, gaining new skills, and sharing what he learns via the Survival Fitness Plan website.

www.SurvivalFitnessPlan.com

amazon.com/author/samfury
goodreads.com/SamFury
facebook.com/AuthorSamFury
instagram.com/AuthorSamFury
youtube.com/SurvivalFitnessPlan